A Storm in a Teacup

DANI BORTOLI

Ordering Information:

Prime Seven Media
518 Landmann St.
Tomah City, WI 54660

Printed in the United States of America

In Dominique's memory.
To everyone who can relate.

INTRODUCTION

I am not the first, and certainly will not be the last to experience the feelings and situations that originated this book, but impressively, in all of them I felt so lonely.

If you are dealing with something that is said to be "a storm in a teacup", it certainly is not. A storm is always a storm. And you may feel, but you are not alone!

Speak up, or like me, write up.

My writings represent structured descriptions of my thoughts and serve as healing mechanisms. Most of my poems and writing pieces came out during severe depressive crisis and symbolises my therapeutic process. This book is a mixture of feminism, politics, and mental health, i.e real life.

I wish that my words touch you and my book to be a game changer, like those which divide us "in before and after", quoting Ryane Leão.

FRIENDLY WARNING

This book contains heavy emotional language which some may find distressing.

Content includes trauma, mental illness, violence, negative cognitions, among other subjects.

If you do not feel ready or if any of these topics are potential triggers, please, <u>stop now</u> or review the table of contents to avoid such topics — *potential triggering topics highlighted with "*".*

In any case, if you are feeling in distress, unwell, in low mood, lack of energy or having negative cognition, help is available. Please, do not wait, talk to someone.

Help available:

- Call **116 123** to talk to Samaritans.
- Call Mind's support line on **0300 102 1234**.

- National Suicide Prevention Helpline UK

  Offers a supportive listening service to anyone with thoughts of suicide. You can call the National Suicide Prevention Helpline UK on **0800 689 5652** (6pm to midnight every day).

- Campaign Against Living Miserably (CALM)

  You can call the CALM on **0800 58 58 58** (5pm–midnight every day) if you're affected by suicide or suicidal thoughts.

TABLE OF CONTENTS

HARD TIMES

THE FINAL STRAW.

02/05/2023

The worst violence is subtle.

Very subtle.

So, you can't even scream.

Do not make noise. No one would listen.

Amazing, but not a priority.

Please, do not create problems.

Do not get credit.

Do not complain.

Smile. Do not make them uncomfortable.

They made me feel like a sucker,

a fool, a complete idiot.

I am suffocating.

I am imploding.

And I am still going.

For another round.

And for only one reason:

Survivorship.

SELF-PORTRAIT *

You think you can go away and start over.
But no, you can't.
Your trauma will follow you. Forever.
You won't trust people.
You will close yourself emotionally.
You will see patterns, everywhere.
You try, but you can't escape.
It is stuck in your mind, and time, only
and slowly, incorporates it into you.
It is deeply embodied, impregnated,
and becomes your identity.
Not even all the love in the world
can heal your trauma.
It will show up subtly.
In your dreams.
In your empty eyes.
In your art.
But you can
Look at it.
Embrace it.
Accept it.

As part of you.

Just a part,

A small part.

You are immensity.

THE PLEASER *

August/2024

I am sorry,

I said.

I honestly did not want

To cause any inconvenience

Of leaving a body behind

To be dealt with.

Or making you uncomfortable

By my urgency to rest.

I'm sorry if I offended your beliefs,

If I disappointed your expectations,

If I had no reasonable reasons.

I'm sorry

If my attempts would bring

trouble to your ward.

If your career would be questioned.

If the health care system would have failed.

I'm sorry if, for a moment,

I just stopped considering all of this.

I'm sorry if, for a moment,

I thought only about myself.

About my pain.

My inability to breathe.

My complete lack of energy.

And decided that it was time to stop.

Life is made up of ups,
downs and rock bottoms.
I wish I could say that rock
bottoms are outliers, unusual.
That people have good character and hearts.
But life would soon contradict me.
I wish I could say "move forward",
keep going, that the path is easy
That "good" still exists and
that justice is done.
But I prefer to be honest and recommend:
Stop fantasizing.
Face life, just as it is.
Hard. Painful, dirty, merciless.
I don't even know if there is a path,
a direction to follow
What comes after tomorrow?
Maybe another rock bottom
And so?
Are you ready?

(ABOUT FANTASY)

I remember clearly the fear I
felt seconds before the act.
I remember the rage I saw
in your furious eyes.
However, I do not remember
the physical pain.
I do not remember the exact moment.
Perhaps because the act itself is irrelevant.
Especially because it was
what left fewer scars.

(PHYSICAL VIOLENCE) *

WHO ARE YOU?

Who am I?

Right?

Who am I?

To question demigods?

I am the Friday afternoon case.

The last-minute resolution.

The less important.

The troublemaker.

The one to be avoided.

The lunatic, the stupid.

The one that can't afford.

The beggar for help.

And so,

Who are you?

To question demigods?

Living doped.

Under control.

Feeling nothing.

Empty eyes.

Full mind.

(ABOUT DEPRESSION)

She was afraid of the world.

But her greatest danger,

Was always

Inside home.

(DOMESTIC ABUSE) *

02/2022

My thoughts

Keep saying:

You are a sucker.

Stupid.

So idiot.

Not good enough.

I wouldn't say

Such things

To my worst enemy.

Why am I saying that to me?

I notice

And I caress my face

In an act of kindness and self-love.

I reassure myself.

I'm not my thoughts.

(NEGATIVE COGNITIONS) *

And now,

Is it again.

Life,

Merciless,

Spills it in my face:

Who I am

Where I came from

The mud

The bottom

Deep down

Where there is nothing

No money

No help

No support

No privilege

No basic needs

No empathy or sympathy

No friendship to recur

Here I am again

On my own.

Exhausted.

But fighting still.

(REALITY)

This is perfect, but it is not a priority.
You are perfect, but not ready yet.
You meet all the requirements,
but you have no personality.
Nice to meet you. Who are you?
What do you do? – Nice to meet you,
I am the one who has worked
with you for four years.
They silence you, make you invisible,
take you out of the priorities,
they want you submissive.
Don't "create" problems, don't speak
loudly, or even better, don't speak at all.
Don't express yourself, don't be
so happy, it gets in the way.
The "supposed" support for diversity
is always blatant, it goes down
well, you know? We *need* that.
Oppression, however, is subtle.
Under the covers, carefully masked.
Images of women and black women
have been used as a way to show that:
yes, we have, want and encourage

women in the job market, as long as
they don't make too much noise.
Give it your all, in silence.
At the background.

(HYPOCRISY)

Don't expect me
To take part
In your theatre
It's been a long time
since I've been where
I don't fit in.
This discomfort
just shows
the abyss
between us
and distance
is the easiest
and only
path
to this coexistence.
Even if I wanted to,
no matter how hard I tried,
this depth is unreachable
and doesn't suit
nor guide me.

(TWO-FACE PEOPLE)

DISCRIMINATION DOES NOT EXIST *

They called me "biased" and suggested I
was "against the law" when I questioned
why the hiring process only selected men,
four in total, and stand for the necessity
of more women to be considered.
None of them are "good enough", they replied.
All men are hired in a fair process,
based exclusively in their own merit.
Women, though, would only be
considered if they were truly
outstanding and, often, overqualified.
CVs:
An acceptable men candidate has
a degree, does not really matter in
what subject, and when they are "very
good", 1 or 2 months of intern roles.
For women, an acceptable candidate
must have a degree, preferably in related-
subjects, at least one more language (but
ideally 2) and, if they have a master, they
can possibly be invited to the interview.

I was threatened – "and if someone sends
your position to the HR?" - As if I would
have any issues to support my point.
Numbers showed who was right, so
much so that it could not be denied.
And then, when my rage and sadness
could no longer be masked, I heard:
"I didn't expect this conversation
to take so long."
What was expected?
Silence and agreement.
Submission.
Of course, as a woman who needs a job,
submission would be the "right" outcome.
Don't expect from me to don't stand
for what I believe in, my answer.
While fighting against gender
discrimination, I have been subjected
to a machismo situation myself.
Do you have any idea where I came from?
Of course, I am in a privileged position now.
But, as soon as I need to change
myself to be in, I am out.
I am selling my workforce, not my
values and what I believe in.

They came

Smiling and friendly.

"We are all a happy family here".

This should have said a lot.

They were invited to contribute.

They came in.

Got something valuable.

They left.

No thanks or goodbyes.

For me, remained:

An endless medical record

And a lot of work to do.

Exhaustion,

Fear,

Judgements

and Doubts.

And after everything,

I am the one to be avoided.

I am the one who needs to prove what I say.

My words mean nothing.

I am the one who needs to explain
My illness.
Or be considered
Irresponsible.

(UNFAIRNESS)

You said:
You settle and you move on.
It is simple.
Right?
But I ask you:
How?
Can you please tell me?
How?
How do I move on?
How can *I* move on?
Can you ensure the agreement
will heal my trauma?
I won't have nightmares.
I will sleep peacefully and finally trust
people again and live happily ever after?
I will suddenly no longer panic
after receiving communications.
My confidence will return as soon
and easily like a magic trick.
Is that easy?
If so, I indeed can move on.
Doesn't seem the, or my, case though.

It's more likely that you have no
clue what mental illness is.
No settlement can make me move on.
Justice, maybe, if this vague concept exists.
Should I give up?
Why is it so hard?
Maybe because means more for me than
you can possibly see or understand.
Maybe it's my dignity that
is on table. Not yours.
Maybe my dignity means
something, at least for me.
It is not about money.
It is about dignity.
And my dignity is not on sale.

(JUST MOVE ON) *

I wish

I could

Talk about love,

Romance,

And beautiful stories.

But

My heart

Is too broken

To think about

Futilities.

(BROKEN HEART)

I'd like to be with you.
I am unable to say it.
I'd like to cry.
I am unable to.

(INABILITIES)

Lengthy texts.

Full of feelings.

Illusions.

Only,

To understand

What you are:

Unmet

Expectations.

(ABOUT ROMANTIC LOVE)

I stopped looking for you,
on the subway lines and at each station.
I'm no longer interested in seeing
your photos, nor trying to find
out what you've been up to.
You're finally gone completely!

(OVERCOMING)

And,

The worst,

Is

To realize,

That the world

Does not

Stop

Because

I am

Ill.

Life

Goes on.

And

Does not

Wait

For me.

(ABOUT ILLNESS)

BETTER TIMES

God is not something that can be explained.

Or you know,

Or you do not!

(FAITH)

I am a woman.
I am light.
And brightness.
I could never
be a shadow.

(BEING A WOMAN)

I was running away from myself.
Fleeing from my own self.
Now I have no choice,
I have to look at, face myself.
And I want to dive in.
I want to know myself so well,
every little piece of me
So that I never again question any of my
decisions, nor doubt any of my perceptions.
So that other people's opinions
about who I am or what I do are
incapable of bothering me.

(HEALING)

OASIS

In the middle of the chaos
There is a place where I can breathe, freely.
I can sleep, with no judgments.
I have been walking in the unknown.
But now I can see.
There is a bridge which separates
the before and the after.
There are good surprises on the way.
There is also fun in the way.
There is peace.
There is "saudade".
There is beauty.
There is love and healing.
There is life, good life, afterwards

FACE YOURSELF

I would say
Look yourself in the mirror
Very deep there
Find who you are
Trust it
Speak of it
Stand up for it
Honour it
Fight for it
Or
You will never
Be able
To look
At the mirror
Again

(Do not avoid yourself)

OCEANS

Respect my tears.

They are oceans.

Please

Do not try to stop them.

As heavy waves will inevitably come to you.

Just let them flow.

Through your shoulder.

Give them space.

To bring everything they carry.

Each tear is a merciful act

allowed by my body.

They are wanted and necessary.

They heal wounds.

Deep pains.

So, please,

Just respect my tears.

MY BIT

Acts of rebellion:

Bralessness.

Ignoring "demigods".

Pretending ignorance.

Being happy, despite everything I see.

I do remember
The punch on my stomach,
That usual uncomfortable feeling
Of tightness and breath holding
When you mentioned
That I should go through my "roots",
Thousands of thoughts for a second
Reminding all the negative things
Painful memories came up
Followed by an ocean of tears
I couldn't and didn't want to control
Staring down.
My head was heavy with all the shame
I carried over the last 34 years
No one judged me though.
Pity eyes have changed to empathetic eyes.
And I could just be myself.
And cry, like a baby, like the baby, like
the child that couldn't cry years ago.
The time has come to face who I am.
And I won't avoid.
I won't escape from me, from who I am.
The healing is in that way.

And I am not giving up on myself.

After all, despite the hard memories, also

good ones arouse, like little beams of light.

Proving that it is not only hell.

There is also love in me,

in my history, in my family.

A kind of love that is not easily recognizable.

Not the kind of love that "sells".

Is the love that requires you to stop,

reflect and pay attention to meanings,

to generations and to "whys".

This love also makes who I am

My values.

(LOVE ALSO BELONGS TO ME)

TO: MOM AND DAD

You are always ahead of your time.
I am very proud of you.
And the more I grow, the
more I see myself in you.
The more I get to know you,
the more I realize that
I am this person because I have you as parents.
I could not be any different.
Our essence,
Our social values,
are the same.
And I am so proud of us.

Art, as well as us, humans, is
perfect in its imperfections.

(ART)

Happiness is
A cat
In my lap
In a cold, cozy day!
Finding comfort
And identity
In a feminist book
Listening to
My favourite song
In a vinyl player
Playing my first song
On my new guitar
Writing
Poems.

(HAPPINESS)

My mom uses to say
That cats "live better"
Because they don't know that they will die.
My aunt says
That cats, once dead, go straight to heaven.
They have no sins.
The purity of thought and belief is genuine.
And it is beautiful how they
think about life and death.
How they judge animals' experiences
with the same logic as humans.
And how would it be to look
through life as animals.
Enjoying the simplest things in life.
A long nap in a cold day, without worries.
Be complete present when in company.
Calmly feel the sunlight warming my face.
Stay curious on anything new.
Take time to rest without questioning
the merits and deservedness' of it.

Just be, purely and naturally, as created.
And being completely honest
about who we are.

(LOGIC AND PERSPECTIVE)

Who is this crazy woman talking about
justice, rainbows, and butterflies?
I am a Revolution.

(ME)